Sing Doun the Mune

Ballads and a Ballad-Essay
by Helen Adam

Edited with an Introduction
by Kristin Prevallet
Foreword by Annie Finch

ISBN: 978-1-7373075-2-5

Introduction © Kristin Prevallet, 2007; 2021.
Book design by Amit Dey
Thanks to Joy Arbor

The mission of Poetry Witch Press is to serve the needs of Poetry Witch Community; to support the resurgence of the Divine Feminine; and to celebrate and share the crafts of meter, form, and rhythm. For more information, please see poetrywitchpress.com

4/28/22

TABLE OF CONTENTS

ESSAY BY HELEN ADAM

FOREWORD

By Annie Finch

In 1983, I heard Helen Adam perform. I was standing in the crowded doorway of the sanctuary of St. Mark's Church in New York's East Village, packed with an overflow crowd for a large group reading. I could hardly believe this small, fierce woman, taking the stage after a parade of poets who appeared mostly male, mostly white, and mostly twice her height. Undaunted and unforgettable, she recited her incantational words in a strong and defiant Scottish accent. Who on earth was she? Nobody else in the doorway had a clue. I didn't know who to ask, and Google hadn't been invented yet. Yet for decades I remembered her and wondered. And finally around 2007, thanks largely to the dedicated work of Kristin Prevallet, the editor of this volume, in bringing Adam and her poems to light, I put two and two together and knew which poet I had been fortunate enough to hear.

What was it about Helen Adam that impressed my twenty-six-year-old self so deeply that I kept that memory close for a quarter century without even knowing her name? It had nothing to do with Adam's idiosyncratic persona, her poems' shocking tales and imagery, or even her larger-than-life, campy stage presence. These qualities weren't terribly unusual among the poets in New York at that time. It was, instead, the gift that renders so many of the poems in this book just as unforgettable now as they were then: her phenomenal ear for poetic music.

Adam's ear is so precisely tuned that, in her best lines, it can be nearly impossible to separate out the different qualities of syntax, word-music (vowel length, assonance, consonance, etc.), accent, metrical pattern, and word rhythm that contribute to an overall effect. In this example from a ballad in this book, "In through the keyhole, elvish bright, came creeping a single hair," notice the exact pitch on the word "in" that the syntax requires, if the sentence is going to make sense. It's as if you need to know exactly how the sentence will end in order to pronounce correctly its first syllable—a situation that, bizarrely and almost indescribably, recreates the very activity being described—with the "hair" of the sentence's last word going "in" its first word. And that's just one word! We have the sinuous threatening sensuousness of the threading *th*'s in "through the," and the short and long *i*s in "elvish bright" twining their way through the progression of consonants that make the lips move from fricative to labial to dental in the space of two syllables as if glinting in a sudden light; and all that takes place even before the truly creepy "creeping" that ends the sentence.

This single line—and there are many just as good in this little book—can be approached like a complete song in itself. If you're used to reading poems aloud, as Adam's are obviously designed to be, your mouth may even salivate slightly as you read the line to yourself and anticipate the pleasure of pronouncing it. If you don't yet have the habit of reading poems aloud, here's an invitation to start: read the same line we just discussed aloud three times in a row. Then find the poem in this book that it comes from and keep on going:

> In through the keyhole, elvish bright, came creeping a single hair . . .

Adam's level of mistressry of the music of poetic language cannot be achieved through reading, or education, or ambition, or even through individual life experience. These things may help, but such a fundamental level of familiarity must be gathered physically from other human beings who carry poems in their bodies—and who, therefore, love and understand the bodies of poems. In Adam's case, her poetic mistressry reflects her roots in the oral traditions of the English language, going back generations and centuries to the traditions of the anonymous "border ballads" grown on the wild edge between England and Scotland. Scholars say these ballads were composed orally by women and then passed on orally through many generations, each generation adding their own variations and contributions. This is how poetry grows and lives in indigenous, oral-based societies on all continents, the same techniques with which ancient poems such as the *Odyssey*, *Beowulf*, *Bhagavad Gita*, and *Kalevala* once began.

Helen Adam carried the precious burden of her poetic roots to the United States and continued to nurture and cultivate those roots throughout her life. And yet she was intensely modern as well. Not only does her gift of a direct connection to oral women's traditions in English bestow an amazing legacy on all of us who use the English language, but she also threw herself passionately into life here, befriending cutting-edge poets such as Allen Ginsberg and Robert Duncan and profoundly affecting the course of twentieth-century poetics, and perhaps new age spirituality as well. Adam is a self-aware poet, a sophisticated poet, and a feminist poet; many of her choices are relevant to us today, for example, as a new generation of feminist writers and filmmakers are reclaiming the horror genre from a feminist perspective.

In the essay on the ballad tradition that Prevallet includes here, Adam makes it clear that she thinks of herself as a magical poet. I also think of Helen Adam as a magical poet, a poetry witch who honors poetry's unique approach to form, rhythm, and language not just an aesthetic or intellectual device but also as an emotional and spiritual and physical necessity. At this time of climate crisis and chronic alienation, I believe a hidden spell is encoded in Adam's stunningly entertaining, creepy, and gripping ballads: a spell embedded in the poems' language and structure itself. This spell offers wisdom regarding the connections between rhythm and meter and the rhythms of breath and body, the rhythms of our lives and relationships, the rhythms of the tides and the seasons. It is a healing spell. And to access it, you need only to read these brilliant ballads aloud.

As I close the foreword to this beautiful book on the hopeful night of a new moon, I feel Adam's spell reaching through me, through us, while I repeat aloud three times:

Sing, women o' the Earth,
Sing doun the mune.

Annie Finch
Bryn Mawr, Pennsylvania
October 2021

INTRODUCTION

Helen Adam's Supernatural Ballad Tradition
By Kristin Prevallet

By her own admission, Helen Adam marched through her life to the beat of her own drummer. She emerged into the world just as the Victorian era was hesitantly giving way to a modern consciousness, fragmented by the shell-shock of World War I's splintering of nations into warring factions. The daughter of a stern Presbyterian preacher growing up in a small village in northern Scotland, she found rebellious solace and nourishment by devouring sensual fairy tales and macabre mysteries. She began writing her own verses while still in primary school and managed to catch the eye of the London literati, who deemed her a prodigy: Faber and Faber published her first book at the age of 14; she was destined for notoriety. She followed that destiny first to London, where she lived for many years, working as a society columnist for *The Weekly Scotsman*. In 1947, she embarked on the journey to New York—with her mother and sister in tow—fleeing a war-ravaged Europe for brighter shores.

Thrift-store chic, erudite, and bohemian, the Adams family (Helen, her mother, and her sister, Pat) gradually made their way west; they arrived in San Francisco in the pivotal year of 1954 just as Jack Kerouac, Allen Ginsberg, Robert Duncan, and Jack Spicer were all actively (albeit with very different end-goals) conjuring exciting literary movements. Helen Adam, now in her early 50s, chanting her ballads and reading everyone's tarot with her red lipstick and decadent thrift-store style, plopped herself right into the middle of these young, über masculine, bohemian, literary *méchants*. They hailed her as a singular source of inspiration: the oracle of poetry itself coming through the ballad tradition.

But she didn't write only ballads. She composed an opera, hundreds of collages, and a film. In 1967, she moved to New York City where she landed on her feet once again. Now in her 60s, she found herself at the center of the burgeoning downtown theater scene happening around the Judson Church, the spoken-word scene happening around the Nuyorican Poets Café and the Poetry Project at St. Mark's Church, and experimental sci-fi salons centered around the great Samuel Delaney.

Her literary and artistic output is impressive. And yet, the collision course of the ballad tradition into 20th-century late-Modernism did not result in Helen Adam being accepted into the canons of literary history. She remains a footnote. She's seen as an eccentric, witchy oddball—only a few who seek her out recognize the genius behind the craft of her rhymed formal poems and wild collages. She rests now between the cracks: too weird for the formalists, and too conventional for the avant-garde.

To help locate Helen Adam, it is useful to understand the ballad tradition that she is so passionately channeling through her life and work. The definition of a ballad has been widely disputed, but most agree that a ballad is essentially a song that tells a story. Ballads are usually highly dramatic, and their plots develop in a series of scenes that "leap" from one situation to another. They are performative and, as Susan Stewart has observed, "have the appearance of tradition speaking through someone. . . . The ballad singer is praised with fidelity, not for originality."

Because it is an oral tradition, the history of ballads is difficult to trace. Since the nineteenth century, ballad scholars have had almost as many opinions regarding points of origin and influence as there are versions of the ballads themselves. The songs were passed down through generations, changing as they survived from century to century until they were written down and "fixed" in time by a plethora of nineteenth-century ballad collectors like Sir Francis Child, who edited the definitive *Scottish and English Popular Ballads*.

The tradition that possessed Adam was the Romantic or Supernatural tradition, and it is generally acknowledged that the northeast region of Aberdeen is the source for most of these types of Scottish ballads. From the twelfth century onward, Aberdeen was a port for trading with Scandinavia.

Through exchange, Norse folktales of subterranean dwarfish spirits, enchanted swords, and bloodthirsty trees found their way into the Scottish imagination. Supernatural ballads like "Tam Lin," which are also influenced by Gaelic folk songs and legends, reflect these Scandinavian themes. Included in Child's collection, some of these supernatural ballads made it to America in the early nineteenth century and wove themselves into the American folk tradition.

Ballad collectors such as Child, while seeming to rescue this oral tradition from oblivion, in fact did the opposite. It is impossible to separate any "real" oral ballad tradition from the history of them that was essentially created by these collectors, who, according to Stewart, "saw the reproduction of past forms as a way of animating a continual and illustrative history of the national literature." And yet, the stories being communicated through ballads, as well as the rhythms they transmit, resist any dogmatic or nationalist interpretation. Folklorist Alan Dundes reveals the refusal at the heart of the ballad tradition to be pinned down or define hierarchical agendas or histories. Dundes traces the manifestations of one ballad from the Child collection, "The Ballad of the Walled-Up Wife," all over the world; he determined that it is only through "the multiplicity of approaches and hence interpretations" that the ballad tradition can be understood.

True to its malleable, shape-shifting form, most of the supernatural British and Scottish ballads that became incorporated into the tradition of American folk songs were stripped of their sexual and/or supernatural elements in favor of a moral or ethical conclusion. But Adam's ballads revel in taboo and tell tales of drama and passion, blood and vengeance. Love is not true until the flesh that inhibits desire is carnivorously devoured from skin to bone. As Kenneth Rexroth said of Joan Baez's singing of old ballads like Barbara Allen, the love that is represented in Adam's ballads is "radically subversive" because it cannot be assimilated by the society. Often telling of lovers who are bisexual, cross-racial, or from opposite sides of the tracks, Adam's ballads praise a kind of love that is lawless, anarchic, and boundless. And consequently, when society (or some other outside force) steps in and tries to impose morality or rationality, murder and mayhem ensue.

Adam embodied her ballads and lived her life through their rhythm. She said she composed her best ballads while riding her bicycle through the streets of San Francisco, finding that the rhythms of the bicycle were in sync with the rhythms of the songs that were coming through her. Indeed, it was this thin line between reality and the world of the ballads that Adam inhabited; although she worked menial jobs, she filled her days with poetry, magic, tarot cards, incantations to the moon, and seeking out fairy caves in Golden Gate Park.

But the fairies she conjures are not Tinker Bell—they are the "duergar" spirits that are central to the supernatural ballad tradition she is transmitting. According to Sir Walter Scott in his introduction to the ancient ballad "Tam Lin," the Duergars are the fairies of the Scandinavian tribes, who lived in the "interior recesses of mountains . . . and are supposed to steal human beings." Like Jack Spicer's Martians and ghosts who share authorship of the poem and, in Peter Gizzi's words, "open the circuitry between the living and the dead," Adam too allowed the Duergars to speak through her via the thin line that separates these realms. In her essay "A Few Notes on the Uncanny in Narrative Verse," Adam writes: "the world of the [Ballads] is almost entirely pre-Christian . . . birds talk to maidens, seals doff their skins and become men, Elf Land is as near as the green wood, and ghosts are real, and as taken for granted, as human beings." Adam walked through the world as if Elf Land were just a blink away, and her ballads reveal the narrative thread that perhaps connects us all to collective realms of an embodied imagination.

True to her personal vision, her ballads and collages often deal with matters of inhabitation, in which otherworldly spirits enter and take over the body. In the introduction to her Acadia Press chapbook *Ballads*, Robert Duncan locates Adam's ballads in the tradition documented by Robert Graves in the *White Goddess*. To Graves, the term ballad comes from ballet, the dance of the coven leader in ancient religious cults in Scotland. "At the heart of these poems," Duncan wrote, referring to Adam, "there is a compulsive beat. It is the pulse the narrative poet contributes in her art to subject the listening intelligence to the story's spell. It is also the feet of ancient dancers tromping around the moon or against the sun." Graves's theories on the ballad's origins have been discounted by scholars and yet, there is something true about the magic he saw emanating from the performance of the ballad form. Certainly, Graves would have had to invent a figure such as Adam to prove his theories. And she, born of the local folk who may indeed have the ballad in their blood, incarnates these ideas.

When performing her ballads, Adam focused on putting her audience under a spell, like the trance of the dancer, and relay a story which, through the persistence of an ancient rhythm, would "give them the grue." Defined best as "a spine-tingling shudder," the grue is a physical reaction to what Emanuel Swedenborg (cited in the epigraph to "The Queen O' Crow Castle") calls the "speech of an angel" as it flows from thought to ear to tongue. The shiver down the spine of the reader or listener is caused when one's body is inhabited by the words or thoughts of "something" from outside.

In this way the *grue* is the *soma* of language, the way that words when woven into rhythm affect the spirit and consciousness of the reader or listener. It is that somatic state cautioned by Robert Duncan when he links the *grue* to a "formal compulsion" connecting the demotic urge of poets to, like dictators, "touch upon terror." But it is that very terror of dictators that is exposed by poets who hold the key to turn language toward human connection and away from the hierarchies that would have us war against each other in service to a malevolent higher power. Duncan clarifies, "It is important then to make clear that this *grue* is in the poem an element in a contained experience. The poem is an event in language, yes, but further, it is an event in the language of poetry, and its consequences belong properly to the occasion of the art." This performative impulse made Adam's strength as a singer and writer of ballads undeniable (even though, as many of her friends have reiterated, she was quite tone deaf).

In Adam's ballads, as in so many of her classic predecessors, there is tension between the mortal and the unworldly, and between the flesh and the spirit. She writes, "love and violent death are closely akin." Like the ballad of "Tam Lin" where the maiden Janet breaks the spell of the fairy queen and rescues her lover, only for him to disappear forever into the clutches of the rapacious queen, the lovers and ghosts in Adam's ballads rarely find corporeal salvation. Partly because the stories she tells involve the triumph of eternal love over earthly desire, the characters in Adam's ballads always present a challenge to the mortal world. The fulfillment of love's energy is realized only in death, and her characters (some willing, some not) transcend their flesh even if they break all sorts of social rules in the process.

Some of her ballads involve women who become possessed by their own inner power, gruesomely kill their domineering and abusive husbands, and live victoriously free in the spiritual realm; others tell of selfish desires that result in evil acts of senseless violence, and passions that are not contained by moral or social constraints. Others tell of men admired in the earthly world for their great strength and beauty whose faith and restraint are tested through amorous encounters with Elfland Queens and Witches. Of course, the love that these beings represent is that which most of the male personas cannot refuse, for it is that of unhindered sexuality: the expansive and wild energy of love. It is their efforts to contain it that result in their gruesome demise. Sometimes, these archetypical stories reflect contemporary reality: the disturbing ballad "Miss Laura" tells a story of a White woman wielding both her will and the police state to seduce and then brutally murder a Black man. That her ballads refrain from moral judgment reveals Adam's belief in "the ancient Eastern notion that life is a cosmic game in which the Eternal plays at becoming all forms and creatures of Time . . . [so] nothing, not even the grimmest of human fate, is at all tragic." This is an unsettling philosophy that seeps through Adam's ballads, and among other things, it reflects the presumption of Whiteness to blur the lines between good and evil as archetypically represented by "dark" and "light," without compassion for the bodies that suffered the "grimmest of human fates."

It is interesting to note that Adam had not actually written in Scottish dialect until she arrived on the San Francisco scene. Partly due to Duncan's and Spicer's romanticization of what they perceived to be her link with ancient sources, Adam became more and more interested in her Scottish heritage. Her usage of Lallan (Scots as spoken in southern and eastern Scotland) in her ballads encouraged her to stray from English prosody into new language patterns and narratives. In a lecture on Scottish poets who drew their inspiration from outside Scotland, the Scottish poet and writer Edwin Morgan writes, "Helen Adam is possibly unique in the sense that she would never have made anything of her poetry, even though she wrote a lot of it, if she remained in her native place. She was a latent poet who needed the jolt of an entirely different environment to bring to the surface what was subterraneanly there."

My favorite example of this is "The Queen O' Crow Castle," written in 1954 and illustrated by the collage artist Jess. The poet Joe Dunn published it as the first in his series of

White Rabbit Chapbooks (others in the series include works by Denise Levertov, Richard Brautigan, and Charles Olson), making it her first publication since the books she published as a child and subsequently renounced. In the poem, Adam uses Scots dialect, which complicates not only the rhythm of the ballads, but the structure and content as well. The ballad is structured to tell two stories simultaneously: the larger story of the pure Castallen, who drives out the devil from the castle of the cursed Queen; and the story of the crows who, after the devil is "cast oot," take over the castle. Like the crows taking over Ginsberg's voice in part five of Kaddish— "Lord Lord Lord caw caw caw Lord Lord Lord caw caw caw Lord"—a chorus of crows echoes and comments on the story as it unfolds.

Helen Adam's is a voice out of time, and the ballad tradition that she passes down through us continues to cast the spell of narratives that tingle up and down our spines. Helen Adam is a singular luminary whose ballads, if you read them out loud and late at night, will sneak into your mind and create phantasmagorias of haunting, vengeful violence cloaked by the sensual lull of the ballad form. And then, as you dream, you'll hear that rhythm, and through it, the earliest beats and rhythms of storytelling. And Helen Adam holds that oracle.

(Amended from the introductions to *A Helen Adam Reader* [www.kprevallet.com/books/a-helen-adam-reader/] and the *Museum Poetica: Neglectorinos* [caesuramag.org/posts/kristin-prevallet-poems-by-helen-adam].)

Works Cited

Adam, Helen, "A Few Notes on the Uncanny in Narrative Verse," *The Poetry Society of America Bulletin* 70 (Spring 1980): 13.

————, *A Helen Adam Reader*, edited and with an introduction by Kristin Prevallet (Orono, Maine: National Poetry Foundation, 2007).

Dundes, Alan, Preface to *The Walled-Up Wife: A Casebook* (Wisconsin: The University of Wisconsin Press, 1996), xi.

Scott, Sir Walter, "Introduction to the Tale of Tamlane: Of the Fairies of Popular Superstition," in *Minstrelsy of the Scottish Border* (London: George G. Harrap & Company, Ltd., 1931), 288–291.

Spicer, Jack, *The House That Jack Built: The Collected Lectures of Jack Spicer*, ed. Peter Gizzi. (Hanover, NH: Wesleyan University Press, 1998).

Stewart, Susan, *Crimes of Writing: Problems in the Containment of Representation* (New York: Oxford University Press, 1991), 112.

For information on the history of the ballad tradition, I have relied on David Buchan's *The Ballad and the Folk* (London: Routledge & Kegan Paul, Ltd., 1972) and "Talerole Analysis and Child's Supernatural Ballads" in *The Ballad and Oral Literature*, edited by Joseph Harris (Cambridge: Harvard University Press, 1991).

SELECTED BALLADS

BY
HELEN ADAM

A TALE BEST FORGOTTEN

Hail! Most Holy ANUBIS.
In a house by a river that lamented as it ran,
Lived a father, and his daughter, and the dog-headed man.
A father, and his daughter, and the dog-headed man!
It's a tale best forgotten, but before the tale began
From the house to the river limped the dog-headed man.
Blood swelled the river before the tale began.
In the garden, in the garden, while the river slowly ran,
Walked the daughter, and her lover, and the dog-headed man.
The daughter, and her lover, and the dog-headed man!
It's a tale best forgotten, but before the tale began
His daughter, by the river that reflected as it ran,
Fed the bones of her lover to the dog-headed man.
Dog Head he was fed before the tale began.

THE WINDS OF SPRING

The winds of spring were blowing fresh;
The weather, warm and fine.
The Wolf sat down to write between
The candles and the wine.
The Wolf wrote to Forget-me-not,
Upon a fair, clean page,
"Where are the heads! Where are the heads
Of the men I slew in rage?

Go burn them in the blowing fire
Beside the sunset sea.
The Law is tiptoe on my trail,
I fear the gallows tree.
I know that for those severed heads
You cared no single jot.
Yet all was done for love of you,
Divine Forget-me-not."

Forget-me-not wrote to the Wolf,
It was her teasing way,
"The heads hang on the berry bush,
And that is where they'll stay.
Yes, that is where they'll stay, dear Wolf,
Till they begin to rot.
So fare you well in London Town,
From sweet Forget-me-not."

The Wolf bit on his great quill pen.
"Infernal jade," he wrote.
"Pull down the heads. Pull down the heads
Or hemp is at my throat.
Go hide the heads. Go hide the heads,
Or sure as skylarks sing
I'll struggle on the gallows tree
To breathe the winds of spring."

Forget-me-not replied, "Dear Wolf, I have not much to say.
The heads are in the river mud
Near where the schoolboys play.
Some likely lad may catch a head
Upon his fishing line.
The winds of spring am blowing fresh.
The weather's warm and fine."

Half frantic was the Wolf, his face
White in the candle flame.
And now his fingers trembled so
He scarce could write her name.
"Of all the heads, of all the heads, I know you loved but one.
Keep Nathan's head, Forget-me-not,
And let God's will be done!"

Forget-me-not wrote calm and quick.
She used a grey goose quill.
"The heads are under churchyard grass
Where they can work no ill.

But I am dancing in the fire
Beside the sunset sea,
With Nathan's head, with Nathan's head,
The head you promised me.

Yes I am dancing in the fire
Beside the sea waves cold.
The King will give for Nathan's head
Its weight in minted gold.
Its weight in minted gold, dear Wolf,
I'll spend it while you swing
Now high, now low, on the gallows tree,
Tossed by the winds of spring."

The Wolf has blotted with his fist
His last impassioned page.
He plunged a pen-knife through his heart
And died in lonely rage.
He wailed aloud, "Forget-me-not!"
Before his soul took wing.
His blood was blown about her head
By all the winds of spring.

I LOVE MY LOVE

From: *The New American Poetry* (Grove Press, 1960)

In the dark of the moon the hair rules.

—Robert Duncan

There was a man who married a maid. She laughed as he led
    her home.
The living fleece of her long bright hair she combed with a
    golden comb.
He led her home through his barley fields where the saffron
    poppies grew.
She combed, and whispered, "I love my love." Her voice like a
    plaintive coo.
Ha! Ha!
Her voice like a plaintive coo.

He lived alone with his chosen bride, at first their life was sweet.
Sweet was the touch of her playful hair binding his hands and
    feet.
When first she murmured adoring words her words did not
    appall.
"I love my love with a capital A. To my love I give my All.
Ah, Ha!
To my love I give my All."

She circled him with the secret web she wove as her strong
    hair grew.
Like a golden spider she wove and sang, "My love is tender
    and true."
She combed her hair with a golden comb and shackled him to
    a tree.
She shackled him close to the Tree of Life. "My love I'll never
    set free.
No, No.
My love I'll never set free."

Whenever he broke her golden bonds he was held with
    bonds of gold.
"Oh! cannot a man escape from love, from Love's hot
    smothering hold?"
He roared with fury. He broke her bonds. He ran in the light
    of the sun.
Her soft hair rippled and trapped his feet, as fast as his feet
    could run,
Ha! Ha!
As fast as his feet could run.

He dug a grave, and he dug it wide. He strangled her in her
    sleep.
He strangled his love with a strand of hair, and then he buried
    her deep.
He buried her deep when the sun was hid by a purple
    thunder cloud.

Her helpless hair sprawled over the corpse in a pale
        resplendent shroud.
Ha! Ha!
A pale resplendent shroud.

Morning and night of thunder rain, and then it came to pass
That the hair sprang up through the earth of the grave, and it
        grew like golden grass.
It grew and glittered along her grave alive in the light of the sun.
Every hair had a plaintive voice, the voice of his lovely one.

"I love my love with a capital T. My love is Tender and True.
I'll love my love in the barley fields when the thunder cloud
        is blue.
My body crumbles beneath the ground but the hairs of my
        head will grow.
I'll love my love with the hairs of my head. I'll never, never
        let go.
Ha! Ha!
I'll never, never let go."

The hair sang soft, and the hair sang high, singing of loves
        that drown,
Till he took his scythe by the light of the moon, and he
        scythed that singing hair down.
Every hair laughed a lilting laugh, and shrilled as his scythe
        swept through.

"I love my love with a capital T. My love is Tender and True.
Ha! Ha!
Tender, Tender, and True."

All through the night he wept and prayed, but before the first
    bird woke
Around the house in the barley fields blew the hair like
    billowing smoke.
Her hair blew over the barley fields where the slothful
    poppies gape.
All day long all its voices cooed, "My love can never escape,
No, No!
My love can never escape."

"Be still, be still, you devilish hair. Glide back to the grave and
    sleep.
Glide back to the grave and wrap her bones down where I
    buried her deep.
I am the man who escaped from love, though love was my
    fate and doom.
Can no man ever escape from love who breaks from a woman's
    womb?"

Over his house, when the sun stood high, her hair was a
    dazzling storm,
Rolling, lashing o'er walls and roof, heavy, and soft, and warm.

It thumped on the roof, it hissed and glowed over every
      window pane.
The smell of the hair was in the house. It smelled like a lion's
      mane,
Ha! Ha!
It smelled like a lion's mane.

Three times round the bed of their love, and his heart
      lurched with despair.
In through the keyhole, elvish bright, came creeping a single hair.
Softly, softly, it stroked his lips, on his eyelids traced a sign.
"I love my love with a capital Z. I mark him Zero and mine.
Ha! Ha!
I mark him Zero and mine."

The hair rushed in. He struggled and tore, but wherever he
      tore a tress,
"I love my love with a capital Z," sang the hair of the sorceress.
It swarmed upon him, it swaddled him fast, it muffled his
      every groan.
Like a golden monster it seized his flesh, and then it sought
      the bone,
Ha! Ha!
And then it sought the bone.

It smothered his flesh and sought the bones. Until his bones
      were bare

There was no sound but the joyful hiss of the sweet insatiable
     hair.
"I love my love," it laughed as it ran back to the grave, its home.
Then the living fleece of her long bright hair, she combed
     with a golden comb.

COUNTING-OUT RHYME

Seven bonnie sisters on an isle in the west:
The youngest was the fairest, and she was loved the best.

Seven wistful sisters hankering tae wed:
On the beach the mocking waves cast up a sailor dead.

The eldest, as she lugged him from the waves whaur they ran,
Said, "A drooned man is better than nae living man.
For a reel i' the munelicht his banes will be braw;
We'll dance hot together while his flesh rots awa."
Six sisters racing, till a boat it was sunk:
The waves cast up a boozing man, reeking, roudy drunk.

Five sisters hustled back, the sixth chose tae bide.
"A brawl, and a buffet, a black eye for a bride!
But a boozing man is better than nae man at my side."

Five siren sisters vividly aflame:
The surges brought a greedy man, he gobbled as he came;

His tusks fast crunching on a muckle fish-tail.
The fifth sister grumbled, "He's as huge as a whale!

He gorges wi' a gusto that is daunting indeed,
But a greedy man is better than nae man tae feed."

Rough waves sprachaling, a man plunging through:
He gripped the fourth sister, and beat her black and blue.
The fourth sobbed, "A cruel man clouts me tae my knees,
But a cruel man is better than nae man tae please."
Three hopeful sisters turning towards the foam:
There came a dull man floating in, as if he floated home.

The third sighed, "A dull man will haver and prate.
He'll harp and carp and din my ear, early and late.
But a dull man is better than nae man tae hate."

Twa bonnie sisters naked in the night,
The cauld waves breaking, the mune shining bright.

The cauld waves breaking, the surf drenching doun:
It rolled in a mucky man on sands like the mune.
He was crusted thick wi' barnacles, tarry from the sea.
He scarted, and he scratched, and he girned in a gree.

"He's mucky as a tousled tyke!" the second sister said.
"But a mucky man is better than nae man in my bed."

The youngest and the fairest, she was alone,
The first star flickering, the seagulls flown.

"A dull man, a dirty man, a drunk man," she said,
"A cruel man, a greedy man, or a drooned man in my bed?

The sea waves may dunk them deep, for I'd refuse them a'.
I'll live alane, and happily, and love nae man at a'."
The cats o' the kirk-yard drifted tae her side.
The hither and thither cats cam' wi' her tae bide.

Wi' cats hurra-purrying and fish swimming slaw
She lived as light-hearted as the sea-breezes blaw.
The waves broke around her wi' a rush and a roar.
They shone in the munelicht but cast nae man ashore.
By sunlicht, and munelicht, they cast nae man ashore.
One sister walking neath a wierd sickle mune:
The waves phosphorescent, the night clear as noon.

A long wave lifting, it birreled as it broke.
The spray frae its flying brow went up like altar smoke.

Then cam' the unicorn, brichter than the mune,
Prancing frae the wave wi' his braw crystal croon.
Up the crisp and shelly strand he trotted unafraid.
Agin' the lanesome lassie's knee his comely head he laid.

Upon the youngest sister's lap he leaned his royal head.
She stabbed him tae the hert, and Oh! how eagerly he bled!

He died triumphant and content, his horn agin' her knee.
The crescent mune fled doun tae meet the phosphorescent sea.

"Seven!" yowled the kirk-yard cats. "Seven!" thrummed the
   breeze.
"Seven!" sang the fish o' yon seraphic seas.
"Seven doomed sisters on an isle in the west:
The youngest was the fairest, and she was loved the best."

NIGHT NURSERY RHYME

Bells clang low in Tom Never's Tower.
High is the moon. Late is the hour.
Fallen lax as a hawthorn spray,
The moon maid lies under flowering may.

The mirror speaks on Tom Never's wa'.
"She was the fairest o' them a'."
The armed man turns where torches pass.
His mailed fist threatens the weeping glass.

Over the hills and far away
The moon doth shine as bright as day.
A silver whispering fills the air.
"She was the fairest o' the fair."

The bells ding fast, and the bells ding slow.
She moves, a wraith in her robes of snow.
Through blossoming thorns, sleep scented may,
Tae the claver o' bells she wafts her way.

Tom Never! Tom Never! Thy mirror is dark,
Save far in its depths a fiery spark.
She hover up, like a deathly flower,
Tae the window high in the wizard's tower.

She seeks the window looking on night,
Beyond the reach o' an eagle's flight.
The great tower swings wi' an earthquake shock.
"When the wind blows the cradle will rock."

The magic egg frae the roof is hung.
Rock-a-bye baby, roughly swung.
The egg rays light frae a hundred eyes.
A light as fierce as its raging cries.

The red rose laughs and the lily flower.
Tom Never laughs in the burning tower,
His arms outstretched as he leaps through light
Tae seize his shadow and clasp it tight.

The shadow flickers between the wa's.
The light o' the unborn leaps and fa's.
Upon the lovers that light is shed
It fa's and leaps tae the dance they tread.

Rich man, poor man, begger man, thief,
Loved alike wi' passion and grief.
A' the King's horses bounding and gone.
How many miles tae Babylon?

His shadow flames in the man's embrace.
The chanting fire is their trysting place.
Against the window the woman clings,
Spreading her wide, snow weighted, wings.

2.

Her palms beat fast on the window pane.
The tears on her cheeks like crystal rain.
She craves, wi' the dead moon's glum desire,
Yon lovers lost in their world o' fire.

"Ride a cock horse!" cries the babe unborn.
"Little Boy Blue come blow your horn."
As hearts are shaken, that tower doth shake
Tae thundering bells that warn "Awake!"

"Awake, or fa' frae the crags o' dream.
Awake or dee wi' the cock's first scream."
As fades the full council gazing on day,
She fades and pines tae a phantom grey.

Broad and cauld are the fields o' dew.
Cauld is the grass her feet lag through.
She sinks tae dust mid the hawthorn grove.
A trumpet sounds for triumphing love.

The road that runs through the starlit sky,
And the riders tae Babylon prancing high.

Their horses rear when the trumpet ca's.
Pitched frae the ceiling the bairnie fa's.

Gang doun, Lord Bothwell, frae Mary's toun.
And Paris frae Troy, gang doun, gang doun.
Not while the day star dwines in the west
Will peace be found on a woman's breast.

The bells are hushed in the burning tower.
The moon lies hid in the hawthorn bower.
The mirror whispers, blind on the wa'
"She was the fairest o' them a'."

THE STEPMOTHER

My lord's young daughter in the earth finds rest.
They laid her doll upon her shrouded breast;
So the waxen image, with its crown of glass,
Is the child's companion under churchyard grass.

I had little liking for that silent child,
With her ways so quiet, and her eyes so wild.
And the first wife's beauty in her wistful face
To stir his memories and mock my place.

She had no playmates and was much alone.
To secret cruelties I will not own.
It was only, only that I could not bear
His smile of pleasure when he called her fair.

This house is older than the old thorn trees.
Its rooms all echo with the roar of the seas.
At night, if a child cried, nobody would hear.
But what should be stirring for a child to fear?

A month of sea mists, and at last, she died.
He knelt down weeping at the new grave side.
My words of comfort stammered into air.
The headstone trembled, and the doll stood there.

My heart beat heavy when its eyes met mine.
Black eyes shining bitter and malign.
He lifted up his head when he heard me groan,
And it darted silently behind the stone.

THE HOUSE O'THE MIRROR

Upon the hill my lover stands.
A burning branch is in his hands.
He stamps impatient on the stane,
And calls and claims me for his ain.

I bolt my door. I hood my light.
I rin tae slam the shutters tight.
I tug my curtains claise and thick.
I stop the clock lest it should tick.

My house is dark. My house is still.
He shines and thunders on the hill.
I pace the rooms, and as I pass
I see myself within the glass.

The glass is tall, and like a gate.
My image watches while I wait
For him tae loup the hill o' night
And raze my house wi' heavenly light.

At his approach I'm like tae dee
Sae hard my hert belabours me.
This house o' stane is frail as straw,
For at a clap its wa's doun fa'.

But wae's my hert for well I ken
He seeks a love ne'er found by men.
Foredoomed, and damned, he seeks the lass
Wha haunts the darkness o' the glass.

The ghaist that in the mirror gleams,
Floating aloof, like one who dreams;
For her he rages, mad and blind,
And plunders a' my flesh tae find.

He dives in flame, and whirls me low
As if tae seize on drifting snow.
He shrieks because he canna clutch
What lies beyond the grief o' touch.

Aye! though we strauchle breast tae breast,
And kiss sae hard we cry for rest,
And daur a' pleasures till they cloy,
We find nae peace, and little joy.

For still between us stirs the shade
That ne'er will lie beneath his plaid.
A' but my ghaist tae him I give.
My ghaist nae man may touch and live.

Oh! mirror like the midnight sky.
Sae high and dark, sae dark and high!

There bides my phantom far frae men,
In warlds nae earthly lovers ken.

My flesh is starvit morn and night
For a' love's horror and delight.
My ghaist apart frae passion stands;
It is my ghaist that love demands.

While blood dunts loud agin' my ear,
And banes grow weak wi' blissful fear,
Upon the hill my lover manes
For what has neither blood nor banes.

KILTORY

Kiltory rode hunting through deep woods and green.
In the kingdom o' Scotland his like ne'er was seen.
Wherever he hunted, by valley or steep,
The hearts o' the youthful like fountains wud leap.

There's many a bonnie lass making sad mane,
"Kiltory has left me at day-break alane.
Oh! why mun he leave wi' the first light o' day?
Kiltory rides hunting though love bids him stay."

Lord Rand's wanton lady, where hill waters flowed,
Caught sight o' Kiltory as hunting he rode.
She saw him jaunt past at the blue break o' day.
"If yon were the huntsman, I'd fain be his prey!"

On the brink o' the river Kiltory rode by.
In the first light o' sunrise his face she did spy.
"Gin I were a falcon tae come at your call,
Frae ramparts o' heaven tae your fist I wud fall."

Lord Rand, frae the Indies, fetched home for his dame,
Rare diamonds like water, and rubies like flame.
"For diamonds and rubies I care na'," she said.
"I would that Kiltory were laid in my bed."

"Oh! what will content ye, my dear lady gay!"
"Alane wi' Kiltory content I wud stay.
I crave for the finest o' a' Earth's delights,
Tae lie wi' Kiltory for ten starry nights."

Kiltory rode hunting in the forest sae green.
And ever behind him, Lord Rand rode unseen.
He saw the sun glint on Kiltory's brown hair.
"Ye micht ha' lived lang gin ye were na' sae fair."

The woodlands were lonely. Lord Rand took a dart,
And struck doun Kiltory cleft clear through the heart.
When evening drew late, tae his lady he said,
"The huntsman, Kiltory, is laid in your bed.

Come hither, my lady, lie doun wi' your dear.
A rival sae braw I ha' reason tae fear.
Come lie wi' your true love for ten starry nights.
I'll grudge ye nae hour o' your stolen delights."

Tae the dead man he flung her. He nailed up the door.
"Kiltory, I wish ye the joy o' your whore!"
Awa in the woodlands the wild throstles cried,
And the waters ran red on the brant mountain-side.

The waters, at morning, run red on the steep.
The wild throstles cry, and the young lassies weep,
For never again, at the blue break o' day,
Will Kiltory ride hunting while love bids him stay.

THE QUEEN O' CROW CASTLE

A BALLAD FOR JESS COLLINS

> *The speech of an angel or a spirit with a man is heard*
> *as sonorously as the speech of a man with a man; yet*
> *it is not heard by others who stand near, but by himself*
> *alone. The reason is because the speech of an angel flows*
> *first into a man's thought, and by an internal way into*
> *his organ of hearing . . . it also flows into the tongue*
> *and excites it in a slight vibration, but not with any*
> *motion, as when the sound of speech is articulated by it*
> *into words by the man himself.*

> —Swedenborg

Haw, craw, craw haw, kra craw crackarus!

In the glen o' Crow Castle the mountain is steep
Whaur groves o' the Goddess grow secret and deep.
Groves o' the Goddess whaur Love doth abide.
There walk the young at the blue even tide.

Callastan alane willna' walk in yon shade,
Nor seek, 'neath the leaves, for a warm, hidden maid.
The finest young man in the length o' the glen
Averteth his face frae the pleasures o' men.

He walks wi' an angel baith morning and night.
The heavens may lour, but he looks tae the light.
He's cared for one lass since his earth life began,
And the Queen o' Crow Castle she cares for nae man.

"Haw!" skreech her corbies, "She cares for nae man!"

Awa up the brae whaur the waterfa's gleam,
Callastan wud fish in the clear shallow stream.
An angel strode by at the first blink o' day,
And to the caught fish heard the fisherman say;

"Oh! fish
Frae the pure springs O morning,
Skinkle agin
In God's water,
Wi' your braw scales
Sae bonnily shining.
Life that I took
For nae reason
But the Deil in my hert,
Be born agin."

The Zodiac's archer is bending his bow.
Sagittarius rises as Taurus sinks low.
Beyond human ken Aphrodite is strong.
Nae man may boast that he mocked her for long.

When the stars o' her glory rise blatant and strong
Nae man alive may resist her for long.

He walked wi' his angel, serenely they talked.
By the tower o' Crow Castle they turned as they walked.
The Queen heard their footfa's disdaining that place.
She leaned frae the tower for a fleet moment's space.
Callastan looked up, and he saw her white face!

He saw, high above him, the face o' the Queen.
A face thistle crowned, in a split second seen.
His hert caught and held twixt the blink o' an ee.
"The Queen o' Crow Castle I'll love till I dee!

I n'er loved till now, but I'll love till I dee!"

Craw, Craw, Callastan, gudebye tae the days
o' strolling wi' angels, exchanging sweet praise.
Tae the Queen o' Crow Castle struck speechless ye'll kneel,
While she shrieks like a cat in the clutch o' her Deil.

Haw, Craw, Ske, Skaw, Haw. She's loved by a Deil!

Black banners beat in the onrushing dark.
Frae the tower o' Crow Castle there flies a red spark.
Rash is the man, when the black banners blow,
Wha weds wi' the Queen o' the Castle o' Crow.

Catching his hand fast, the angel cries, "No!
Wed not the Queen o' the Castle o' Crow!"

Ka, Croakarorom, the Castle o' Crow!

"Seven as husbands, ha' entered her tower,
Lain in the dark by that lass like a flower.
Always, at morning, the Queen lies her lane.
Naught left o' the man but a fire brackled bane.
Shuddering ash, and a fire brackled bane.
And a wild crowd o' crows whaur the Queen lies her lane.

Locked is her chamber, and guarded her bed.
The Deil is stark naked wha straddles its head.
The monster is naked as jealous desire.
Her seven braw husbands he's blasted wi' fire.

Fire,
        Fire,
            Fire fierce and red.
The gay fires o'danger in the dark o' her bed.

Light in the grass that nae een can endure!
The fish frae the water brook brawling and pure,
At the touch o' the angel revived frae the dead.
Twa hands were clasped o'er its quicksilver head.

There's many a lass wi' Callastan wud bide,
But the angel o' Paradise stalks by his side.
The wings reared above him vibrate wi' bright rings.
Nae lassie daur step 'neath the stir o' those wings.

"Callastan, Callastan, but women are fair.
In groves o' the Goddess their beauties they bare.
They're paler than star beams. They're dark as the storm.
Cauld flits the dew yet their bodies are warm."

"I walk wi' an angel. His garments are spun
o' rays frae the hert o' the black hidden sun.
He smiles when I speak, and his face shines sae clear
The beauty o' women I've nae nead tae fear.

I walk wi' an angel, I follow his tread.
By bridges o' fire over wide gulfs o' dread.
I watch while he wrestles celestial despair.
The sorrow o' women I've nae nead tae share."

Haw! scream her corbies. Their wings swak the air.

"Chieftains and princes expected delight.
The maiden untouched in the dark marriage night.
Grand were those gallants, and sure o' their bliss.
Ho! they died in her Deil's mou' afore the first kiss!"

Ha! Kea! Crackarus, afore the first kiss!

Frae ramparts above her the black banners stream.
Crow Castle is rocked by the strength o' her dream.
A thunder cloud mounting makes drummly the skies.
When forked lightning flashes the Deil grips her thighs.

Shrieking and skirling her crows ride the skies.
Haw, Haw, Hozannah! They're riding the skies.

Ashes, and dust whaur her young lovers lay.
Banes in the bride bed before break o' day.
Seven dead husbands! I'm telling ye true.
Callastan tak heed lest the eighth ain be you!

Eight croak her corbies. *The eighth wull be you.*

Ain, twa, three, four, five, six, seven, Craw!
Swakked doun, bogle bit, caught up skirlin', banes brackled,
Skulls crunched, clapper clawed, dunted.
Dust and ashes, dead gone, dead gone.
Kra, craw,
  clap, slap,
    eight wull be you.

"Though seven he's murdered, the eight I mun be.
Though her chamber be locked, though the lock ha' nae key,
Though held tae her Deil's hert I hear her laugh low.
I'll strike doun her door wi' a stunnering blow.

What e'er lurks behind it, I'll rive doun her door.
Aye though she be ten times the Deil's mocking whore.
I'll beat frae her chamber that Prince in his pride.
And I'll be the first man tae wake by her side.

The first man, at morning, tae wake by her side!"

Caw, Crax, and Rax, shriek her crows wheeling high.
Throw the fish in the fire, and the cursed fiend will fly.
The marvelous fish frae the bricht springs o' day
For the Queen o' Crow Castle as ransom ye'll pay.

Haw, crack a raw! What a ransom ye'll pay!

The heavens were darkened and fu' o' strange cries.
The twa heard the crying and felt their hair rise.
In silence they hastened, through night wi' nae star.
They came tae her tower, and the door stood ajar.

Wheesht, Wheesht, the dead went before.
Seven dead husbands ha' opened her door.
Kra!
Wheesht, wull ye wheesht. We'll drink o his gore.
Sharpen your beeks,
Kra! Kra!
If he opens her door.

The door was ajar, and it cracked as they came.
Claise tae the threshold a mouth breathing flame.
Merciless lightning split open the night,
And Love was revealed in that instant o' light!

Blind, blazing Love in that instant o' light!

Kra, Kra, Ha-a-a!

The menacing angel thrust open her door.
Frae Tweed tae Euphrates men heard the Deil roar.
Wings weighted wi' thunder thrashed over the bed,
And the lassie shrieked once wi' her hands tae her head.

The arm o' the angel her demon cud thole,
But not the sharp stench o' the fish on the coal.
By reek o' its blessing distracted and drowned
Tae deserts o' Egypt he fled, and was bound.

Bound, bound, dunted and bound.
By the might o' the angel the monster was bound.

In deserts o' Egypt his lust did'na tire.
The deserts o' Egypt he scorched wi' his fire.
That sun shaking fury she will'na forget.
Till the end o' a' love nights her Deil she'll regret.

Craw, Kra, crackarus. Kra, Ha! swirlin' fast.
The love that is pure. Ha, Ha, is the love that will last.
Frae the hert o' the woman yon angel did weel,
Kra croakarorum, tae cast oat the Dei!

Tae Egypt,
    Auld Egypt.
       Auld,

           Auld,

              Egypt.
                  Haw, Craw!
                He cast oot her Deil!

The Queen o' Crow Castle leads doun intae night
Callastan, her new love, that creature o' light,
They move in the mirk as the moon and the sun,
Compelled tae their love since the planet first spun.

The man and the woman are naked and lone.
His angel awa, and her Deil overthrown.
Who then prevaileth? Who taketh that tower?
Hushed is the night, and the lass like, a flower.

Rash is the mortal wha plucketh that flower!
Kra, Kra, crackarus, wha plucketh that flower!

Smoke reeking black on the blue morning sky.
Over his ashes her gorged corbies fly,

Mair than the Deil must a man overthrow
Wha weds wi' the Queen o' the Castle o' Crow.

Great cry her corbies. They reel as they go.
Great is the Queen o' the Castle o' Crow.

Great is the Queen. Kra! Ha! o' the Castle o' Crow!

THE BIRKENSHAW

Silver and braw is the Birkenshaw
In the rush o' the springtime breeze.
Bonnie they grow up Badenoch,
Those circling silver trees.

None daur eater the Birkenshaw
For dread o' the elfin Queen.
The silver trees are that Lady's place
Sae high up Badenoch green.

The Elf Queen bides in the Birkenshaw,
A fountain o' ice her crown.
She leads the hunt when the hills open,
Riding the young men down.

Spurred wi' fire gae her hunting maidens
Through mists o' the haunted glen.
Slung at their hips are silver daggers
Athirst for the herts o' men.

Ill befalleth the young herdsmen
Strayed frae the moorland track,
Wha hears the horns in the mist blowing
And the elf hounds at his back.

But gin a lad ha' bonnie grey een,
Or maybe a gorse-gold head,
Some fairy maid may beckon him tae
Her lanely heather-bell bed.

Their Queen has a hert like a crystal wave,
A wave o' the murderous sea.
She'll ha' nae mercy on any young man
Nat matter how braw he be.

It was the harper Robin o' Leith
Wi' his great harp in his hand,
He's up and awa tae the Birkenshaw
In the green uncanny land.

At the first note o' the harp music
He played in the land o' the Queen,
She's started up in a shaft o' sunlicht
And glittered afore his een.

"What are ye doing, human harper,
Breaking the Elf Queen's law,
Playing your harp up Badenoch
In the magic Birkenshaw?"

"I pluck my harp in the Birkenshaw
Where the silver branches blow,
Far they mind me of the running waves
When I harped Atlantis low."

"I'll gae ye gold tae spend, Robin,
And a gold crown for your head,
If ye will enter my hollow mountain,
And harp whaur my feast is spread."

"I will na' harp for your gold, Lady,
Nor yet for a kingly crown.
The speech o' my harp can never be bought
Though the hollow hills tumble down."

"Rash man! You're a rash man, Robin.
Tae a strong god ye mun pray,
That ye look in the face o' the Queen o' Faery
And daur tae my her nay!

Saddle and bridle your steeds, my maidens,
We'll hunt in the high moonlight,
Over, and under, and galloping
By the cock o' the steeple o' light.
I'll hae the head o' that proud poet
Or ever I sleep this night.

Flourish your whips, my fairy maidens.
Fasten your spurs o' fire.
If the hunters ride, and the hunted runs,
Ha! Ha! wha'a the first tae tire?"

A' the hosts o' the Elf Queen riding,
And one man running alone.

Round the mountain the horses raced
Till the sparks spat firm the stone.

He's changed his shape tae a white owl flying
Awa tae the moorland springs,
But she knew the owl was Robin o' Leith
By the moonglow on his wings.

He's changed his shape tae a tom cat cursing
The rival o' his desire.
But she knew that tom was Robin o' Leith
By his crossed eyes kindled fire.

"Ride fast, ride fast, my fairy maidens.
Brandish your whips and ride.
The cunning poet, the shape changer,
Frae me he shall na' hide."

He's changed his shape tae a circling eagle,
And a league-long swimming seal.
But whaurever he fled, in earth or heaven,
The hunt was at his heel.

High as the stars her horns were blowing.
In the deeps he could na' drown.
He's plunged back intae the Birkewhaw,
And there they ran him down.

"Bid fareweel tae your harp, Robin,
Snap its strings wi' your hand.
For I will keep ye a thousand years
In my silent fairy land."

"The strings o' my harp are strong, Lady.
The strings o' my harp are strong.
My harp has ridden a doomsday wave
Wi' a mane a rainbow long.

When I have broken its strings, Lady,
The floods o' my hert will flow,
As once they flowed for the truth o' love
When I harped Atlantis low."

He's broken those harp strings clean and quick.
The moon shone broad and chill
As the great harper the Queen had got
Strode intae the hollow hill.

She's seized on him wi' her arms sae cauld
But he melted frae her clutch.
He's changed his shape tae the holy harp,
And that she daur na' touch.

His sangs flew up like birds about her
And blinded her wi' their wings,

Till his banes became the base o' the harp
And his hert became its strings.

The harp stands in her hollow mountain,
And whiles the harp will sing.
Pure and strong is the harp's voice
Wi' nane tee pluck a string.

The harp utters the truth o' love,
And tae a' the host that hears
A thousand years are but a day,
And a day a thousand years.

MEMORY

*Certain sylvan spirits who dwell in forests, or in great
solitary trees.*
—Fraser, *The Golden Bough*

The house was built in the tree's shade.
The tree was old when the house was made.

The man and woman, and their young child,
Came to the lonely house in the wild.

They loved each other. Their hearts beat free
Beneath the shade of the haunted tree.

The tree and the house stood high on a hill.
A great valley unearthly still

And veiled at evening in mist like snow,
With its fields and rivers lay far below.

The fair young woman and her loved son
Played 'neath the tree till dusk was gone.

They lingered under its branches old.
They kissed each other with lips night cold;

While slowly dying colors of day
From the great valley faded away.

And to his mother the child said,
"If I were living when you were dead,

Oh! lovely mother, beneath this tree,
Would you come in secret to comfort me?"

"If you were living, and I was dead,.
And I could wake in the dark," she said,

"My eyes not sealed, and my lips not dumb,
Be sure, my darling, that I would come."

A lonely spirit lived in the tree.
The oak tree older than all men be.

Through long forgotten dead centuries
The oak grew slowly to monstrous size;

While in the silence beneath its boughs
The priests of the Sun God whispered vows.

For many and many an ancient year
The oak was holy and held in fear.

Adored and dreaded in worship then
By generations of mortal men.

Long past, but still, on the lonely heights
Above the valley on moonlit nights

The tree remembered how long ago
Came white robed druids through mist like snow.

The tree remembered the dagger's gleam
The solemn chanting. the victim's scream.

And how the blood leapt vital and red
Till the roots of the sacred oak were fed.

Through nights of silence, and days of sighs,
The tree remembered the sacrifice.

It saw the woman walk with the man
As walked true lovers since time began.

It saw those parents play with the child,
Three souls alone in the silent wild.

But on its branches, and round its roots
They wreathed no garlands, and hung no fruits.

No smoke of incense stirred on the air.
There came no murmur of evening prayer.

The oak, long holy and held in dread,
Stood with its branches darkly spread.

Its shadow moved like a boundless flood.
It saw the three and desired their blood.

Long days of summer to autumn ran,
The shadow touched the mind of the man.

And he grew weary, and frowned to see
The springing fires of the mighty tree,

That towered in glory and put to shame
His love's uncertain and fading flame.

The red leaves fell, and the year grew late.
The heart of the man was black with hate.

He loathed his life, and his weary mood.
And the one who loved him in solitude.

And when he listened he seemed to hear
A voice in the last leaves whisper clear.

It said, "She holds you against your will."
The moon rose high and the night was still.

He led his wife to the oak tree root,
The heart in his breast like a black fruit.

The leaves above them were almost still,
They breathed, "She holds you against your will.

Take up your dagger, and slay her now."
Said the last leaves on the cold bough.

He took his dagger, as if impelled.
To the roots, in shadow, the warm blood welled.

At the roots, in shadow, the woman sank.
The leaves sighed, and the tree drank.

The blood was offered. The man was free,
He dug a grave close under the tree.

He did her low in the earth, and crept
Barefoot to bed while the child slept.

And in the morning, he told the child,
How walking late in the moonlit wild

The woman wandered, and lost her way.
And alone together they two must stay.

She might return with the spring, he said.
But the child, in horror, thought, She is dead!

Yet spoke no word of the truth he knew.
The days passed, and the child grew.

A time came, though it came not soon.
A still night of the full moon.

On his cold pillow the boy awoke.
He thought he heard a voice that spoke.

He fled through shadow, and ran barefoot
Through long grass to the tree's root.

The leaves moved softly above his head.
"Is love forgotten?" the leaves said.

"Is love forgotten, that used to be
So deep, so dark, between you and me?"

The tears of the orphan fell like rain.
"Oh! Mother!" he cried "Have you come again?"

He kissed the trunk of the tree night cold.
"Are you the mother I loved of old?"

"Yes, I your mother still love you true."
And on his body the leaves rained dew.

"A deed on Earth remains to be done.
Avenge, avenge me, my mortal son.

Upon a mound under moonlit skies.
Look. deeply sleeping, my slayer lies.

Take up his dagger. and kill him there."
Said the lonely spirit evil and fair.

The child listened, and could not tell.
That the mother who once had loved him well,

In death lay silent, while this that spoke
Was the soul alive in the age old oak.

The soul the Druids had feared and fed
With blood fresh leaping, and warm, and red.

How could he vision, or how suppose.
When dew fell chilly, when mist arose

And tilled the vile with a white flood.
The ghost in the great tree dreamed of blood.

And stirred, and thirsted, with craving sighs.
To drink the wine of the sacrifice.

Around the bole of the oak he crept
To the low mound where the man slept.

He felt no pity to spare or save.
The man lay stretched on the woman's grave.

He took the dagger, and stabbed him deep.
He gave the sleeper eternal sleep.

The blood gushed forth, to the roots it sank.
And deeply, gladly, the tree drank.

But no sweet wraith came offering joy,
Nor kiss of peace to the awe-struck boy.

No shining phantom drew near to bliss.
He felt, in horror, his loneliness.

He felt the silence.
He sensed the sound of blood fast sinking into the ground.

He saw the thirsting, primeval tree.
He saw, and trembled, and turned to flee

Far down the valley, where mist might hide
His head from the dark boughs vast and wide.

He fled light foot, but he felt his sin
Like a magic circle that ringed him in.

At early dawn, when the dew appeared.
He came once more to the place he feared.

He came once more to his huge desire.
The house of his youth he set on tire.

He burned the house, and his father's flesh.
A prince in the world of loneliness

He lived remote, and mad in the wild.
And he would laugh like a careless child,

And climb high up in the radiant dome
Of the oak tree palace, his only home;

And swing all day in its branches strong,
And drown its voices with crazed sweet song.

His laughter echoed like bells rung shrill
Both night and day on the silent hill.

And those who heard it, far down the vale,
Crossed themselves while their cheeks grew pale.

A time came, though it came not soon,
A still night of the full moon.

He took the dagger, now dark with rust,
Deep in his heart the blade he thrust.

He died with laughter still on his mouth.
The tree, for the last time, slaked its drouth.

Time blows like wind o'er the grassy lea,
And alone on the green hill lives the tree.

And strangers notice no more, no less,
Than a tree alone in the wilderness,

Than a ruined cottage with fire black stones,
And a tittle circle of fragile bones.

But legend whispers, and all men fear
To leave the valley and venture near.

Yes, even birds in the wild wood free,
Avoid the shade of that ancient tree.

When deep in silence the world is drowned,
No wild thing moving, no voice, no sound,

But the winter wind in the vaulted sky,
When the time of the old, old, rites draws 'nigh;

Then beneath the starry, enormous skies,
The tree spirit trembles and cries.

The frozen branches where no leaves cling,
Lift their arms to the dark and sing

A song of lust in the blood's dark praise.
The wind blows, and the stars blaze.

The green voice, terrible, and divine,
Roars its thirst for the sacred wine.

MISS LAURA

Black, black, black, is the color of my true love's hair.

—Traditional song

"Black is the color of my true love's skin.
White girl, black man, where is the sin?"
Sweet talk murmured by Miss Laura's mouth.
Lynch fires howling up and down the South!

Up the avenue gentlemen ride.
Want Miss Laura for their golden bride.
Ladies so pretty don't grow on trees.
Rich men, poor men, down on their knees.

Rich men, poor men, every man white.
Miss Laura, lovely as the morning light,
Who will you choose to take to your bed?
"The black boy standing at my horse's head."

Ancient avenues, and haunts of gloom.
Miss Laura's riding with her dark groom.
Riding slowly under shrouds of moss
To the brimming river that the dusk blows across.

They walk their horses in the sundown glow,
Beside Savannah where it ripples slow.

Hear what she whispers in her muted voice,
And tell me truly if that man had a choice?

Oh! tell me truly if that man had a choice?

"Look, my Honey, on Savannah's wave,
Still be flowing when we lie in the grave.
Lovers walking in the future's light,
Will care no longer if they're black or white.
Oh! care no longer if they're black or white.
Love me Honey, where Savannah flows.
Love me naked.
Throw away my clothes.
My body's open, and I want you in.
Black is the color of my true love's skin."

Early morning when the white men came,
Running in packs, and carrying flame.
She heard them running, then she shrieked, and said,
"Black boy forced me to his savage bed!
Forced Miss Laura to his jungle bed!"

They lit the faggots, and the flame licked high.
He cried "Miss Laura!" with his last loud cry.
For her was the last wild glance of his eyes.
'Ere the blare of his burning shook the sun from the skies!
Black man burning shook the sun from the skies!

Miss Laura's talking, and she can't keep still.
From her pretty lips the love words spill.
Talking, talking, with a tongue of fire
That must speak passion and can never tire.
Folk who wander by that river's brink,
Just when the red sun's aiming to sink,
Under the branches where the moss moves slow,
Hear Miss Laura speaking hoarse and low.

"Love me, Honey, where Savannah flows.
Love me naked. Throw away my clothes.
My body's open, and I want you in.
Black, black, black, black is the color
Of my true love's skin!"

CHEERLESS JUNKIE'S SONG

Seeking love upon a day,
A day of summer's pride,
I left Long Island's suburbs
For the Lower East Side.

The train it roared and thundered,
And I sang above its scream,
There's a cockroach coming towards me
But it cannot spoil my dream.

Love! Love! and L.S.D.
It shall not spoil my dream.

Blue moonlight over Thompkins Square.
"Drop out, tune in, turn on."
The village all around me,
And Long Island's suburbs gone.

In a pad far down on Fourth Street
Soon I welcomed the approach
Of the rat that loves the twilight,
And the nimble footed roach.

Love! Love! at eventide,
The grey rat and the roach.

I'm always where the action is.
I blow my mind all day.
While on Long Island's tennis courts
The bland suburbans play.
And I was born suburban!
Who would ever credit that?
No chick who saw me frugging
With the cockroach and the rat.

It's Ho! for Horse, or methedrine
To spark the swinging mood.
While rats run up my trouser leg
Roaches share my food.
Rats and roaches nuzzle me
When its dark and hot.

Love! Love! It's all the same
Mixing Speed and Pot.
First a rat, and then a roach,
Or both as like as not.
If I can't find a fix tonight
My marrow bones will rot.

Goodbye transcendent Thompkins Square I haven't long to stay.
A double jolt of heroin and I'll be on my way.
Let rats and roaches bury me.
They'll bury me in state,
As they march from Verrazano Bridge Down to the Golden Gate,

Clear across the continent.
Yonder let me lie,
In the gutters of Haight Ashbury,
To freak the passers by,
Till all the tourists gape, and say,
"Brother! He died high!"

Let rat tails write my epitaph.
Brother! He died high!

MUNE RUNE

Sing, women o' the Earth,
Sing doun the mune.
When a' seas are motionless,
Then will she droon.

Yon jealous virgin,
Auld in heaven serene;
Spying on Earth's lovers
Wi avid een.

Forge me a black dirk
Tae fling at the sky.
Weave me a spider's web
That will float sae high.

Sing, women o' the Earth,
Sing doun the mune.
Sisters, she's bound tae fa'
Sudden and soon

His lane let the lordly sun
In the heavens move
Till not a hert on Earth
Remembers love.

Frae every breaking wave
Her wierd we'll dree.
Droon, droon the goddess
In her ain siller sea,

Never tae lure agin
The unborn tae the breast.
Then shall a' women laugh
And the seas rest.

And there shall be
No more moonlight.
And there shall be
No more moonlight.

And there shall be
No more opposites
Over a' the Earth.

ANAID SI TAERG (GREAT IS DIANA)

Moondoom ! Moondoom ! Moondoom !
Anaid si Taerg. Anaid, Anaid,
Noom, noom, Moondoom !

Begone evil moon.
Run howling from heaven.
Run howling, panic to Earth.
Crash to splinters on the polar ice.
Die strangled in the hair of the north wind.

Skull riding the sky,
Empress of dream we deny you.
Seven times seven
Times we turn
Away from your mirror
Distorted and tarnished.

Blind light, blow out.
Now the wings of your elves wither.
The spears fall from the hands of your huntresses.
Your cats vanish
Over all the Earth.

Angel, bland, implacable,
Reigning serene over agony,

Wafted through heaven
By the shrieks of the mad,
Now cry, now cry, run howling.

There'll be no more peace in the lunar nights.
The jets wil follow the rocket flights.
They'll be signs saying "Eat at Edie's Place"
On the biggest craters of the full moon's face.

Guardian of silence, it won't be long
'Ere you get an earful of games and song.
The World's Series will be all relaid.
And your glaciers tremble to the Hit Parade.

Moondoom ! Moondoom ! Moondoom !
Anaid, Anaid, Ah !

Horns, horns, blow for the moon's mort!
Ancient enchantress your nymphs forsake you.
The dogs of the Tarot will tear you to pieces.
The sun's fist shatters your face of grief.

Sing women o' the Earth
Sing down the mune.
When a' seas are motionless
Then will she droun.

Yon jealous virgin
Auld in heaven's serene,

Spying on Earth's lovers
Wi' avid een.

Forge me a black dirk
Tae fling at the sky.
Weave me a spider's web
That will float sae high.

Sing women o' the Earth
Sing down the mune.
Sisters she's bound tae fa'
Sudden and sune.

His lane let the lordly sun
In the heavens move
Till not a heart on Earth
Remember love.

Frae every breaking wave
Her wierd we'll dree.
Droun, droun the goddess
In her ain siller sea.

Never tae lure agin
The unborn tae the breast.
Then shall a' women laugh,
And the seas rest.

And there shall be no more moonlight.
And there shall be no more moonlight.
And there shall be no more opposites
Over all the Earth.

WITCHES RIDING SONG

Ware, Haunt, awa!
Ware, haunt, awa!
Loup my steed,
Stamp and speed,
Gang till the green stars fa'.
Carry me over tae Blokula,
Tae the blessed meadow of Blokula.
Follow the moon tae Blokula.
Ware, haunt, awa!

Come up Soloman, Javen, Dolovan,
Drac, Sandtander, Pytho.
Rear my stallion,
Rush my darlin' one.
Up my Tommy cat, go.
Ware, Haunt, awa!
Hoo , and talon, and paw.
Carry me over now. Carry me over now.
Ware, Haunt, awa!

TRANSFORMATIONS

I am Red the rose.
I am Silver the sea.
I am Blue the sky.
I am Green the grass.
Names, names,
Fated to be
For a little while
And forever to pass.

I am Thorn the rose.
I am Drown the sea.
I am Storm the sky.
I am Graves the grass.
Names, names,
Fated to be.
I am Love the moon,
But I too must pass.

I am Black the sun
In a heaven hidden
Except from dreams
That the great drugs keep.
My heart's blood falls
On a world forbidden.
Beware, lost dreamers

Who dream so deep
That you transcend sleep.

I am out beyond.
In my rays are shaken
Universes and Gods undone.
Who dreams of me once
He shall not waken
Even to death.
I am Black the sun.

A FEW NOTES ON THE UNCANNY IN NARRATIVE VERSE

BY
HELEN ADAM

(Excerpt. Originally published in "The Poetry Society of America Bulletin," Vol LXX, Spring 1980.)

As a writer who has always loved narrative poetry, and the world of the weird and the so-called supernatural, I am glad to offer a few notes on these enthusiasms. I am going to restrict myself only to poems I knew and loved as a child, because then the combined power of poetry and magic was especially strong.

The appeal of narrative verse goes back to childhood. The first poems I remember from my childhood were story poems. One of these, which still seems magical to me, was Edward Lear's "The Jumblies," which is a deeply mysterious narrative poem. I have not space to quote it all, but the first and last verses seem to make a complete poem in themselves.

from THE JUMBLIES

> They went to sea in a Sieve, they did
> In a Sieve they went to sea,
> In spite of all their friends could say
> On a winter's morn and a stormy day
> In a Sieve they went to sea.
> And when the Sieve turned round and round
> And everyone cried "You'll all be drowned!"
> They only replied "Our Sieve ain't big,
> But we don't care a button we don't care a fig
> In a Sieve we'll go to sea."

Far and few, far and few,
Are the lands where the Jumblies live.
Their heads are green, and their hands are blue,
And they went to sea in a Sieve.

And in twenty years they all came back
In twenty years or more.
And everyone said "How tall they've grown
For they've been to the Lakes and the Torrible Zone
And the hills of the Chankly Bore."
And they drank their health, and gave them a feast
Of dumplings made of beautiful yeast.
And everyone said "If we only live
We too will go to sea in a Sieve
To the hills of the Chankly Bore."

Far and few, far and few
Are the lands where the Jumblies live.
Their heads are green, and their hands are blue,
And they went to sea in a Sieve.

Lear, by the way, was the twentieth child in his Victorian household, and nobody wanted him, not even his mother, yet if he had not lived the world would have lost not only "The Jumblies" but the magnificent "Dong with the Luminous Nose," "The Owl and the Pussy Cat," and all his other inspired and magical creations.

Another great Victorian, Lewis Carroll, also dominated my childhood. Before I could read, I used to weep every time "The Walrus and the Carpenter" was read aloud to me, because I was so sorry for those poor trusting little oysters. I followed them in imagination every step of that fatal walk—and what a long walk it seemed—along the enchanted beach, that beach of solemn loneliness and unearthly beauty, where dwelt the monstrous Walrus, and the pitiless Carpenter, who, as Alice observed, "were both very unpleasant characters." Carroll's "The Hunting of the Snark," with its dazzling wit and hinted horror, outdoes the Surrealists at their own game.

When I got a little older, I was practically brought up on the Bible and the Border Ballads of Scotland. Many of the Old Testament stories are like savage ballads in themselves, and the world of the Border Ballads is almost entirely pre-Christian, with its stern "eye for an eye, and tooth for a tooth" sense of revenge, and its wonderful come-and-go with Nature. Birds talk to maidens, seals doff their skins and become men, Elf Land is as near as the green wood, and ghosts are as real, and as taken for granted, as human beings.

CLARK SAUNDERS

> Clark Saunders and May Margaret
> Walked ower yon garden green;
> And deep and heavy was the love
> That fell thir twa between.

"A bed, a bed," Clark Saunders said,
"A bed for you and me!"
"Fye na, fya na," said May Margaret,
"Till anes we married be."

"Then take the sword frae my scabbard,
And slowly lift the pin;
And ye may swear, and safe your aith,
Ye ne'er let Clark Saunders in."

"And take a napkin in your hand,
And tie up baith your bonny een;
And ye may swear, and safe your aith,
Ye saw me na since later yestreen."

It was about the midnight hour,
When they asleep were laid,
When in and came her seven brothers,
Wi' torches burning red.

When in and came her seven brothers,
Wi' torches burning bright;
They sayd, "We hae but ae sister,
And behold her lying with a knight!"

Then out and spake the first o' them,
"I bear the sword shall gar him die!"
And out and spake the second o' them,
"His father has nae mair than he."

And out and spake the third o' them,
"I wot that they are lovers dear."
And out and spake the fourth o' them,
"They hae been in love this mony a year."

Then out and spake the fifth o' them,
"It were great sin true love to twain."
And out and spake the sixth o' them,
"It were shame tae slay a sleeping man."

Then up and gat the seventh o' them,
And never a word spak he;
But he has striped his bright brown band
Out through Clark Saunders' fair body.

Clark Saunders he started, and Margaret she turned
Into his arms as asleep she lay;
And sad and silent was the night
That was atween thir twae.

And they lay still and sleeped sound,
Until the day began to daw;
And kindly she to him did say,
"It is time, true-love, you were awa."

But he lay still and sleeped sound,
Albeit the sun began to sheen;
She looked between her and the wa'
And dull and drowsie were his een.

Then in and came her father dear,
Said, "Let a' your mourning be;
I'll carry the dead corpse to the clay,
And I'll come back and comfort thee."

"Comfort weel your seven sons,
For comforted I will never be;
I ween 'twas neither knave nor loon
Was in the bower last night wi' me."

The clinking bell gaed through the town,
To carry the dead corpse to the clay.
And Clark Saunders stood at May Margaret's window,
I wot an hour before the day.

"Are ye sleeping, Margaret" he says
"Or are ye waking presently?
Give me my faith and troth again,
I wot, true-love, I gaed to thee."

"Thy faith and troth ye sall never get,
Nor our true love shall ever twin,
Until ye come within my bower
And kiss me cheek and chin."

"My mouth it is full cold, Margaret,
It has the smell now of the ground;
And if I kiss thy comely mouth
Thy days of life will not be long.

O cocks are crowing on merry middle-earth.
I wot the wild fowls are boding day;
Give me my faith and troth again,
And let me fare me on my way."

"Thy faith and troth thou shall na get,
And our true love shall never twin,
Until ye tell what comes of women
I wot, who die in strong travelling?"

"Their beds are made in the heavens high,
Down at the foot of our good Lord's knee,
Weel set about wi' gillyflowers,
I wot sweet company for to see."

Then she has ta'en a crystal wand,
And she has stroken her troth theron,
She has given it him out at her shot-window
With many a sad sigh, and heavy groan.

"I thank ye, Marg'ret, I thank ye Marg'ret,
And aye I thank ye heartilie;
Gin ever the dead come for the quick,
Be sure Marg'ret I'll come for thee."

It's hosen and shoon, and gown alone,
She climbed the wall and followed him,
Until she came to the green forest,
And there she lost the sight o' him.

"Is there ony room at your head, Saunders,
Is there ony room at your feet?
Is there ony room at your side, Saunders,
Whaur fain, fain, I wad sleep?"

"There's nae room at my head, Marg'ret,
There's nae room at my feet.
My bed it is full lowly now,
Amang the hyngry worms I sleep.

"Cauld mould is my covering now,
But and my winding sheet;
The dew it falls nae sooner down
Than my resting place is weet.

"But fair Marg'ret, and rare Marg'ret,
And Marg'ret o' veritie,
Gin ever ye love another man
Ne'er love him as ye did me."

Part of this great ballad's power is the matter-of-fact manner in
which the supernatural is treated. Clark Saunders is murdered
by the sinister seventh brother, but then,

the clinking bell gaed through the town
To carry the dead corpse to the clay.
And Clark Saunders stood at May Margaret's window,
an hour before the day—

And we believe it, and believe the dialogue between the ghost and the girl. And how warm, how comforting, the glow of those gillyflowers growing in "the heavens high," when the poor girl, fearing she may be pregnant, asks of her lover the fate of women who die in childbirth; how vivid the blaze of the torches the revengeful brothers carry, how the simple statement:

> "A bed, a bed," Clark Saunders said,
> "A bed for you and me!"

expresses such great physical passion, which many a modern poet of the "tell everything about sex till you put your reader to sleep" school could not achieve with pages of over-explicit description.

Another ballad in which the mysteries of sex and the supernatural are explored is "Tam Lin."

TAM LIN
> "O I forbid you, maidens a'
> That wear gowd on your hair,
> To come or gae by Carterhaugh,
> For young Tam Lin is there.
>
> "For even about that knight's middle
> O' siller bells are nine;
> And nae maid comes to Carterhaugh
> And a maid returns again."

Fair Janet sat in her bonny bower
Sewing her silken seam,
And wished to be in Carterhaugh
Amang the leaves sae green.
She has braided her yellow hair
A little abune her bree,
And she has kilted her green kirtle
A little abune her knee,
And she's awa tae Carterhaugh
As fast as she can hie.
She had'na pu'd a rose, a rose,
A rose but barely ane,
When up and started young Tam Lin,
Says, "Lady, let alane."

"What gars ye pu' the rose, Janet?
What gars ye break the tree?
What gars ye come tae Carterhaugh
Without the leave o' me?"

"Weel may I pu' the rose" she says,
"And ask no leave at thee,
For Carterhaugh it is my ain,
My daddy gave it me."

He's ta'en her by the milk-white hand
And by the grass-green sleeve,
He's led her tae the fairy ground
At her he asked nae leave.

He's led her tae the fairy ground
Amang the leaves sae green,
And what they did I canna' tell
The green leaves were between.

Janet has kilted her green kirtle
A little abune her knee,
And she has snooded her yellow hair
A little abune her bree,
And she is to her father's ha'
As fast as she can hie.

But when she came tae her father's ha'
She looked sae wan and pale,
They thought the lady had gotten a fright
Or with sickness she did ail.

Four and twenty ladies fair
Were playing at the ba'
And out then came fair Janet
Ance the flower amang them a'.

Four and twenty maidens fair
Were playing at the chess,
And out then came fair Janet
As green as onie glass.

Out then spak' an auld grey knight
Lay owre the castle wa',
And says, "Alas! fair Janet,
For thee we'll be blamed a'."

"Hauld your tongue ye auld-faced knight.
Some ill death may ye die.
Father my bairn on whom I will
I'll father nane on thee.

"O if my love were an earthy knight
As he is an elfin gay,
I wad 'na gie my ain true love
For any laird that ye hae.

"The steed that my true love rides on
Is fleeter nor the wind;
Wi' siller he is shod before
Wi' burning gold behind."

Out then spak her brother dear,
He meant tae do her harm;
"There grows a herb on Carterhaugh
Will twine you an' the bairn."

Janet has kilted her green kirtle
A little abune her knee,
And she has snooded her yellow hair

A little abune her bree,
And she's awa tae Carterhaugh
As fast as she can hie.

Shc had'na pu'd a leaf, a leaf,
A leaf but only twae,
When up and started young Tam Lin,
Says, "Lady, thou's pu' nae mae.

"How dar ye pu' a leaf," he says,
"How dar ye break the tree?
"How dar ye scaith the babe?" he says,
"That's between you and me?"

"O tell me, tell me, Tam," she says,
"For His sake that died on tree,
If ye were ever in holy chapel
Or sain'd in Christentie?"

"The truth I'll tell tae thee, Janet,
A word I winna' lee;
A knight me got, and a lady me bore
As well as they did thee.

"Roxburgh he was my grandfather,
Took me with him tae bide;
And ance it fell upon a day
As hunting I did ride,

"There blew a wind out o' the north
A bleak wind and a snell,
A drowsiness came over me
And frae my horse I fell;
The Queen o' Fairies she took me
In yon green hill to dwell.

"And pleasant is the Fairy Land
For those that in it dwell,
But ay and every seven years
They pay the tithe tae Hell,
And I'm sae fair and fu' o' flesh
I fear 'twill be mysell.

"This night is Halloween, Janet,
The morn is Hallowday;
Then win me, win me, and ye will,
For weel I wot ye may.

"The night it is gude Halloween,
The fairy folk do ride,
And they that wad their true love win
At Miles Cross they maun bide."

"But how should I ye ken, Tam Lin,
How should I ransom you,
Amang a pack of uncouth knights
The like I never saw?"

"You'll do you down to Miles Cross
Between twelve hours and ane,
And fill your hads wi' the holy water
And cast your compass roun'.

"The first company that passes by
Say na and let them gae;
The next company that passes by,
Say na, and do right sae;
The third company that passes by
Then I'll be ane o' thae.

"O first let pass the black, Lady,
And syne let pass the brown
But quickly run to the milk-white steed,
Pu' ye his rider down.

"For some ride on the black, Lady,
And some ride on the brown,
But I ride on a milk-white steed,
A gowd star on my crown;
Because I was an earthly knight
They gave me that renown.

"My right hand will be gloved, Lady,
My left hand will be bare.
And thae's the tokens I gie thee,
Nae doubt I will be there.

"Ye'll tak my horse then by the head,
And let the bridle fa',
The Queen o' Elfland she'll cry out
'True Tam Lin he's awa!'

"They'll turn me in your arms, Lady,
A lizard, and a snake,
But hauld me fast let me nae gae,
Tae be your warldis make.

"They'll turn me in your arms, Lady,
But and a deer so wild;
But hauld me fast, let me na gae,
The father o' your child.

They'll shape me in your arms, Lady,
A hot iron at the fire,
But hauld me fast, let me na go,
To be your heart's desire.

"They'll shape me in your arms, Janet,
A mother-naked man;
Cast your green mantle over me
And so will I be won."

Janet has kilted her green kirtle
A little abune her knee,
And she has snooded her yellow hair

A little abuen her bree,
And she on to Miles Cross
As fast as she can hie.

About the dead hour o' the night
She heard the bridles ring;
And Janet was as glad of that
As any earthly thing.

And first gaed by the black black steed,
And syne gaed by the brown,
But fast she grips the milk-white steed,
And pu'd the rider down.

She's pu'd him frae the milk-white steed
And let the bridle fa'.
And up there rose an eldritch cry,
"True Tam Lin he's awa!"

They shaped him in her arms twa
A lizard and a snake,
But aye she grips and hau'ds him fast
To be her warldis mate.

They shaped him in her arms twa
But and a deer sae wild;
But aye she grips and hau'ds him fast
The father o' her child.

They shaped him in her arms twa
A hot iron at the fire,
But aye she grips and hau'ds him fast
To be her heart's desire.

They shaped him in her arms at last
A mother-naked man.
She cast her mantle over him
And so her love she won.

Then up spak the Queen o' Fairies
Out o' a bush o' broom,
"She that has ransomed young Tam Lin
Has gotten a stately groom."

Out then spak' the Queen o' Fairies
And an angry woman was she.
"She has ta'en awa the bonniest knight
In a' my company.

"But what I ken this night, Tam Lin,
Gin I had kent yestreen,
I had ta'en out thy heart o' flesh
And put in a heart o' stane.

"And adieu, Tam Lin, but gin I had kent
A Lady had ransomed thee,
I had taken out thy twa grey e'en
And put in twa e'en o' tree.

"Had I the wit, yestreen, yestreen,
That I have coft this day,
I had paid my tithe seven times tae Hell
Ere you had been won away."

This ballad, which through a lifetime has never ceased to enchant me, seems to prove the truth of the old saying,

If a man tells you he has seen the Fairies, look
       if he be shaken,
If he be not terrified be sure he has not seen.

For the Fairies of ancient Scotland were not the playful and mischievous elves of England; they were dangerous, proud, often terrible spirits, akin to the Pagan gods of the heath and the forest. And though they could, at times, be capriciously friendly toward mortals, it was often fatal for a human being to have anything to do with them. For a long period after the official acceptance of Christianity in Scotland, the gods of the green-wood and the grim, savage glens remained profoundly real, at least for the country people. And the great festivals like Halloween, when the doors between the worlds stood ajar, continued to be celebrated with more joy and abandon than any Christian ceremony.

In our abominable mechanized civilization, it is hard to realize what it meant to those people of the past to live so near to the fathomless green-wood and the haunted hills seen today in lonely parts of Scotland, the atmosphere of an unearthly world, within a hair-breadth of the world we see, can be overpowering the world of the Earth Goddess, the irresistible Elf Queen, who spoke "out of a bush of broom" as God spoke from the Burning Bush in the Bible. Tam Lin would never have willingly left her enchanted world had he not been afraid of being sent as "tithe to Hell."

At the ballad's ironic and unexpected end, the Elf Queen cries to him,

> "I had paid my tithe seven times tae Hell
> Ere you had been won away!"

The reader is left wondering how long Janet, for all her beauty and bravery, will be able to hold Tam Lin on Earth or quench his memories of that Queen.

For me, the two lines climaxing Janet's wait for the approaching riders and her lover—

> About the dead hour o' the night
> She heard the bridles ring

—are among the most magical in all literature. These are only rivaled by those verses in "Thomas the Rhymer" when True Thomas, also in the Elf Queen's thrall, rides with her into Fairyland.

O they rade on and further on,
And they waded rivers abune the knee,
And they saw neither sun nor moon
But they heard the roaring of the sea.

It was mirk, mirk, night,
There was nae star light,
And they waded through red blood to the knee,
For a' the blood that's shed on earth
Rins through the springs o' that country.

Blood is abundantly shed in the ballads, and shed with passion, and usually without regret.

"O Earl Brand I see your heart's blood."
Ay laly, a lily laly.
"'Tis na' but the glint o' my scarlet hood."
All i' the night sae early.

Some ballads, like "Edward, Edward," imply, rather than tell, a terrible story. But usually the story develops straightforwardly, and often with haunting overtones. Everywhere love and violent death are closely akin. I can recall only one instance in all the Border Ballads where any regret is shown for murder, in the shining verses of the grim "Edom o' Gordon." The young daughter of a defeated chieftain has been lowered, in order to escape, over the hall of a besieged castle, but falls on the point of Gordon's spear.

> Then wi' his spear he turned her owre;
> O gin her face was wane!
> He said, "Ye are the first that e'er
> I wished alive again."

> He turned her ower,
> and ower again; o gin her skin was white!
> "I might ha' spared that bonnie face
> To hae been some man's delight."

Christina Rossetti's "Goblin Market," with its exquisitely varied music and disturbing, sensual beauty, is still the greatest narrative poem ever written by a woman. I was about twelve years old when I first read Coleridge's "The Rime of the Ancient Mariner." I can still recall the shock I felt when the Mariner, having told how the Albatross followed the ship beyond the Arctic ice, trusted the friendly sea men, and came to them "everyday for food and play," pauses suddenly, and the Wedding Guest cries:

> "God save you Ancient Mariner
> From the fiends that plague thee thus
> Why lookst thou so?"

and the Mariner answers,

> With my cross bow
> I shot the Albatross!

I felt instantly the appalling weight of that crime, its unforgivable, wanton cruelty, and was convinced—as I still am—that the Mariner deserved his awful penance. His crime was symbolic of the evil race of man, the long, long history of hideous cruelty toward all the beautiful and innocent living creatures who share the planet with us. Personally, I believe that the dark atomic dangers we now face, which may eventually destroy our world, are caused partly by a karmic residue from such cruelties.

Tennyson wrote such masterful narrative poems as "The Lady of Shalott," "The Lotus Eaters," "Rizpah," and "Morte D'Arthur," which he later included in "The Idylls of the King," where its triumphant pure poetry shames the pallid verse of the rest of those Idylls. Of course, they contain fine passages—Tennyson's extraordinary visual imagery, unmatched in English till the advent of Robert Duncan, insures that—but I cannot abide the transformation of the great King Arthur of legend, and of Malory's rendering, into a smug Victorian gentleman, wearing, in one of Tennyson's most deplorable lines, "the white flower of a blameless life," and capable of that preposterous speech to Queen Guenevere, lying repentant at his feet, in which he tells her windily how flawlessly good and above reproach he is. A classic of the holier-than-thou mentality.

Or worse. One would have thought that the inspired poet who wrote

> O, hark, O, hear! how thin and clear,
> And thinner, clearer, further going!
> O, sweet and far from cliff and scar
>> The horns of Elfland faintly blowing.

would have been the very man to bring to life the great magician Merlin and Vivien, his enchantress, in old age. But the episode of "Vivien and Merlin" is an exercise in almost intolerable tedium. Merlin becomes a prosy old bore, and Vivien, "that creature to enchant a sorcerer," is no better than a suburban shrew. Nothing remains but the spell.

Ah! yes, "the spell of woven peace and of waving hands." That is the magic itself.

For me, Tennyson's masterpiece of narrative verse that conjures up the weird is "Maude," a disturbing, lovely, and profound adventure into horror and madness, which contains, without ever disturbing the narrative's flow, some of the loveliest lyrics. The critics of his day attacked "Maude," but it was Tennyson's favorite among his works, and he enjoyed reading it aloud.

A magical ballad, somewhat in the manner of Tennyson, is
"Keith of Ravelston" by the now almost forgotten poet Sydnel
Dobel. Though certainly sentimental, it has a most haunting
charm for me, especially the refrain, "Oh Keith of Ravelston,
The sorrows of thy line!" which has the power of a spell.

KEITH OF RAVELSTON

>The murmur of the mourning ghost
>That keeps the shadowy kine;
>Oh Keith of Ravelston,
>The sorrows of thy line!

>Ravelston, Ravelston,
>The little path that leads
>Down the golden morning hill
>And through the silver meads;

>Ravelston, Ravelston,
>The stile beneath the tree,
>The maid that kept his mother's kine
>The song that sang she!

>She sang her song. She kept her kine.
>She sat beneath the thorn,
>When Andrew Keith of Ravelston
>Rode thro' the Monday morn.

>His henchmen sing, his hawk bells ring
>His belted jewels shine!

Oh, Keith of Ravelston,
The sorrows of thy line!

Year after year, where Andrew came
Comes evening down the glade,
And still there sits a moonshine ghost
Where sat the sunshine maid.

Her misty hair is faint and fair
She keeps the shadowy kine.
Oh! Keith of Ravelston,
The sorrows of thy line!

I lay my hand upon the style,
The style is lone and cold.
The burnie that goes babbling by
Says nought that can be told.

Yet, stranger, here, from year to year
She keeps her shadowy kine.
Oh, Keith of Ravelston
The sorrows of thy line!

Step out three steps where Andrew stood—
Why blanch thy cheeks for fear?
The ancient style is not alone
'Tis not the burn I hear!

> She makes her immemorial moan
> She keeps her shadowy kine,
> Oh Keith of Ravelston
> The sorrows of thy line!

When I was a child, I read James Thomson's "City of Dreadful Night" as if it were a dark fairy tale, caring nothing for its philosophy of despair and its raging against God, but enthralled by the nightmare city, and the slow, sonorous music of the words that created it.

James Thomson, born in 1834, had a tragic and tormented life. He spent his childhood in an orphanage for seamen's children. At the age of 18, while working in Ireland, he met the beautiful daughter of a sergeant. He fell madly in love with her when she was only 13, and after her untimely death at 15, her image haunted his poetry. His life, in which he pursued various careers, ended in chronic drunkenness and melancholia.

"The City of Dreadful Night," published in 1874, is a long poem, hypnotic in its power. It captivated my mind as a child; and, though I disagree with its philosophy of hopeless misery and helpless fury against the Creator of the universe, I am still moved by its gloomy images, and the way it depicts the terrors of the ill-omened industrial age, the darkness of those huge cities of England, and the dreadful plight of their poor.

Who is most wretched in this dolorous place?
I think myself, yet I would rather be
My miserable
My miserable self than He than He
Who formed such creatures to His own disgrace.
The vilest thing must be less vile than Thou
From whom it had its being. God and Lord!
Creator of all woe and sin, abhorred,
Malignant, and implacable!
I vow
That not for all Thy power furled and unfurled,
For all the temples to Thy glory built,
Would I assume the ignominious guilt
Of having made such men in such a world.

Magnificent but mistaken. The poet's rageful expression is a consequence of his belief in the Western idea that human beings are individuals. However, if the ancient Eastern notion that life is a cosmic game in which the Eternal plays at becoming all forms and creatures of Time is true (and I believe it is), then nothing, not even the grimmest of human fate, is at all tragic.